# The Scholar-Gipsy

## Matthew Arnold

A Phoenix Paperback

*Selected Poems* by Matthew Arnold
first published by J. M. Dent in 1993

This abridged edition published in 1996 by Phoenix,
a division of Orion Books Ltd,
Orion House, 5 Upper St Martin's Lane, London WC2H 9EA

Cover illustration: *Sleeping Shepherd – Morning*,
by Samuel Palmer, Fitzwilliam Museum, Cambridge
(Bridgeman Art Library, London)

ISBN 1 85799 654 2

Typeset by CentraCet Ltd, Cambridge
Printed in Great Britain by
Clays Ltd, St Ives plc

# Contents

## The Forsaken Merman

Come, dear children, let us away;
Down and away below!
Now my brothers call from the bay,
Now the great winds shoreward blow,
Now the salt tides seaward flow;
Now the wild white horses play,
Champ and chafe and toss in the spray.
Children dear, let us away!
This way, this way!

Call her once before you go –
Call once yet!
In a voice that she will know:
'Margaret! Margaret!'
Children's voices should be dear
(Call once more) to a mother's ear;
Children's voices, wild with pain –
Surely she will come again!
Call her once and come away;
This way, this way!
'Mother dear, we cannot stay!
The wild white horses foam and fret.'
Margaret! Margaret!

Come, dear children, come away down;
Call no more!
One last look at the white wall'd town,
And the little grey church on the windy shore;
Then come down!
She will not come though you call all day;
Come away, come away!

Children dear, was it yesterday
We heard the sweet bells over the bay?
In the caverns where we lay,
Through the surf and through the swell,
The far-off sound of a silver bell?
Sand-strewn caverns, cool and deep,
Where the winds are all asleep;
Where the spent lights quiver and gleam,
Where the salt weed sways in the stream,
Where the sea-beasts, ranged all round,
Feed in the ooze of their pasture-ground;
Where the sea-snakes coil and twine,
Dry their mail and bask in the brine;
Where great whales come sailing by,
Sail and sail, with unshut eye,
Round the world for ever and aye?
When did music come this way?
Children dear, was it yesterday?
Children dear, was it yesterday
(Call yet once) that she went away?

Once she sate with you and me,
On the red gold throne in the heart of the sea,
And the youngest sate on her knee.
She comb'd its bright hair, and she tended it well,
When down swung the sound of a far-off bell.
She sigh'd, she look'd up through the clear green sea;
She said: 'I must go, for my kinsfolk pray
In the little grey church on the shore to-day.
'Twill be Easter-time in the world – ah me!
And I lose my poor soul, Merman! here with thee.
I said: 'Go up, dear heart, through the waves;
Say thy prayer, and come back to the kind sea-caves.
She smiled, she went up through the surf in the bay.
Children dear, was it yesterday?

Children dear, were we long alone?
'The sea grows stormy, the little ones moan;
Long prayers,' I said, 'in the world they say;
Come!' I said; and we rose through the surf in the bay
We went up the beach, by the sandy down
Where the sea-stocks bloom, to the white-wall'd town
Through the narrow paved streets, where all was still,
To the little grey church on the windy hill.
From the church came a murmur of folk at their prayers
But we stood without in the cold blowing airs.
We climb'd on the graves, on the stones worn with rains
And we gazed up the aisle through the small leaded
    panes

She sate by the pillar; we saw her clear:
'Margaret, hist! come quick, we are here!
Dear heart,' I said, 'we are long alone;
The sea grows stormy, the little ones moan.'
But, ah, she gave me never a look,
For her eyes were sealed to the holy book!
Loud prays the priest; shut stands the door.
Come away, children, call no more!
Come away, come down, call no more!

Down, down, down!
Down to the depths of the sea!
She sits at her wheel in the humming town,
Singing most joyfully.
Hark what she sings: 'O joy, O joy,
For the humming street, and the child with its toy!
For the priest, and the bell, and the holy well;
For the wheel where I spun,
And the blessed light of the sun!'
And so she sings her fill,
Singing most joyfully,
Till the spindle drops from her hand,
And the whizzing wheel stands still.
She steals to the window, and looks at the sand,
And over the sand at the sea;
And her eyes are set in a stare;
And anon there breaks a sigh,
And anon there drops a tear,

From a sorrow-clouded eye,
And a heart sorrow-laden,
A long, long sigh;
For the cold strange eyes of a little Mermaiden
And the gleam of her golden hair.

Come away, away children;
Come children, come down!
The hoarse wind blows coldly;
Lights shine in the town
She will start from her slumber
When gusts shake the door;
She will hear the winds howling,
Will hear the waves roar.
We shall see, while above us
The waves roar and whirl,
A ceiling of amber,
A pavement of pearl.
Singing: 'Here came a mortal,
But faithless was she!
And alone dwell for ever
The kings of the sea.'

But, children, at midnight,
When soft the winds blow,
When clear falls the moonlight,
When spring-tides are low;
When sweet airs come seaward

From heaths starr'd with broom,
And high rocks throw mildly
On the blanch'd sands a gloom;
Up the still, glistening beaches,
Up the creeks we will hie,
Over banks of bright seaweed
The ebb-tide leaves dry.
We will gaze, from the sand-hills,
At the white, sleeping town;
At the church on the hill-side –
And then come back down.
Singing: 'There dwells a loved one,
But cruel is she!
She left lonely for ever
The kings of the sea.'

## from *Empedocles on Etna*

The out-spread world to span
A cord the Gods first slung,
And then the soul of man
There, like a mirror, hung,
And bade the winds through space impel the gusty toy.

Hither and thither spins
The wind-borne, mirroring soul,
A thousand glimpses wins,

And never sees a whole;
Looks once, and drives elsewhere, and leaves its last
      employ.

The Gods laugh in their sleeve
To watch man doubt and fear,
Who knows not what to believe
Since he sees nothing clear,
And dares stamp nothing false where he finds nothing
      sure.

Is this, Pausanias, so?
And can our souls not strive,
But with the winds must go,
And hurry where they drive?
Is fate indeed so strong, man's strength indeed so poor?

I will not judge. That man,
Howbeit, I judge as lost;
Whose mind allows a plan,
Which would degrade it most;
And he treats doubt the best who tries to see least ill.

Be not, then, fear's blind slave!
Thou art my friend, to thee,
All knowledge that I have,
All skill I wield, are free.
Ask not the latest news of the last miracle,

Ask not what days and nights
In trance Pantheia lay,
But ask how thou such sights
May'st see without dismay;
Ask what most helps when known, thou son of
Anchitus!

What? hate, and awe, and shame
Fill thee to see our time;
Thou feelest thy soul's frame
Shaken and out of chime?
What? life and chance go hard with thee too, as with us;

Thy citizens, 'tis said,
Envy thee and oppress,
Thy goodness no men aid,
All strive to make it less;
Tyranny, pride, and lust, fill Sicily's abodes;

Heaven is with earth at strife,
Signs make thy soul afraid,
The dead return to life,
Rivers are dried, winds stay'd;
Scarce can one think in calm, so threatening are the
Gods;

And we feel, day and night,
The burden of ourselves –

Well, then, the wiser wight
In his own bosom delves,
And asks what ails him so, and gets what cure he can.

The sophist sneers: Fool, take
Thy pleasure, right or wrong.
The pious wail: Forsake
A world these sophists throng.
Be neither saint nor sophist-led, but be a man!

These hundred doctors try
To preach thee to their school.
We have the truth! they cry;
And yet their oracle,
Trumpet it as they will, is but the same as thine.

Once read thy own breast right,
And thou hast done with fears;
Man gets no other light,
Search he a thousand years.
Sink in thyself! there ask what ails thee, at that shrine!

What makes thee struggle and rave?
Why are men ill at ease? —
'Tis that the lot they have
Fails their own will to please;
For man would make no murmuring, were his will
        obey'd.

And why is it, that still
Man with his lot thus fights? –
'Tis that he makes this *will*
The measure of his *rights*,
And believes Nature outraged if his will's gainsaid.


Couldst thou, Pausanias, learn
How deep a fault is this;
Couldst thou but once discern
Thou hast no *right* to bliss,
No title from the Gods to welfare and repose;


Then thou wouldst look less mazed
Whene'er of bliss debarr'd,
Nor think the Gods were crazed
When thy own lot went hard.
But we are all the same – the fools of our own woes!


For, from the first faint morn
Of life, the thirst for bliss
Deep in man's heart is born;
And, sceptic as he is,
He fails not to judge clear if this be quench'd or no.


Nor is the thirst to blame.
Man errs not that he deems
His welfare his true aim,

He errs because he dreams
The world does but exist that welfare to bestow.


We mortals are no kings
For each of whom to sway
A new-made world up-springs,
Meant merely for his play;
No, we are strangers here; the world is from of old.


In vain our pent wills fret,
And would the world subdue.
Limits we did not set
Condition all we do;
Born into life we are, and life must be our mould.


Born into life! – man grows
Forth from his parents' stem,
And blends their bloods, as those
Of theirs are blent in them;
So each new man strikes root into a far fore-time.


Born into life! – we bring
A bias with us here,
And, when here, each new thing
Affects us we come near;
To tunes we did not call our being must keep chime.

Born into life! – in vain,
Opinions, those or these,
Unaltered to retain
The obstinate mind decrees;
Experience, like a sea, soaks all-effacing in.

Born into life! – who lists
May what is false hold dear,
And for himself make mists
Through which to see less clear;
The world is what it is, for all our dust and din.

Born into life! – 'tis we,
And not the world, are new;
Our cry for bliss, our plea,
Others have urged it too –
Our wants have all been felt, our errors made before.

No eye could be too sound
To observe a world so vast,
No patience too profound
To sort what's here amass'd;
How man may here best live no care too great to
explore.

But we – as some rude guest
Would change, where'er he roam,
The manners there profess'd

To those he brings from home
We mark not the world's course, but would have *it*
            take *ours*.


        The world's course proves the terms
        On which man wins content;
        Reason the proof confirms
        We spurn it, and invent
A false course for the world, and for ourselves, false
            powers.


        Riches we wish to get,
        Yet remain spendthrifts still;
        We would have health, and yet
        Still use our bodies ill;
Bafflers of our own prayers, from youth to life's last
            scenes.


        We would have inward peace,
        Yet will not look within;
        We would have misery cease,
        Yet will not cease from sin;
We want all pleasant ends, but will use no harsh means;


        We do not what we ought,
        What we ought not, we do,
        And lean upon the thought

That chance will bring us through;
But our own acts, for good or ill, are mightier powers.


Yet, even when man forsakes
All sin – is just, is pure,
Abandons all which makes
His welfare insecure, –
Other existences there are, that clash with ours.


Like us, the lightning-fires
Love to have scope and play;
The stream, like us, desires
An unimpeded way;
Like us, the Libyan wind delights to roam at large.


Streams will not curb their pride
The just man not to entomb,
Nor lightnings go aside
To give his virtues room;
Nor is that wind less rough which blows a good man's
        barge.


Nature, with equal mind,
Sees all her sons at play;
Sees man control the wind,
The wind sweep man away;
Allows the proudly-riding and the foundering bark.

And, lastly, though of ours
No weakness spoil our lot,
Though the non-human powers
Of Nature harm us not,
The ill deeds of other men make often *our* life dark.


What were the wise man's plan? –
Through this sharp, toil-set life,
To work as best he can,
And win what's won by strife. –
But we an easier way to cheat our pains have found.


Scratch'd by a fall, with moans
As children of weak age
Lend life to the dumb stones
Whereon to vent their rage,
And bend their little fists, and rate the senseless ground,


So, loth to suffer mute,
We, peopling the void air,
Make Gods to whom to impute
The ills we ought to bear;
With God and Fate to rail at, suffering easily.


Yet grant – as sense long miss'd
Things that are now perceived,
And much may still exist

Which is not yet believed –
Grant that the world were full of Gods we cannot see;

All things the world which fill
Of but one stuff are spun,
That we who rail are still,
With what we rail at, one;
One with the o'erlabour'd Power that through the
            breadth and length

Of earth, and air, and sea,
In men, and plants, and stones,
Hath toil perpetually,
And travails, pants, and moans;
Fain would do all things well, but sometimes fails in
            strength.

And patiently exact
This universal God
Alike to any act
Proceeds at any nod,
And quietly declaims the cursings of himself.

This is not what man hates,
Yet he can curse but this.
Harsh Gods and hostile Fates
Are dreams! this only *is* –

Is everywhere; sustains the wise, the foolish elf.

Nor only, in the intent
To attach blame elsewhere,
Do we at will invent
Stern Powers who make their care
To embitter human life, malignant Deities;

But, next, we would reverse
The scheme ourselves have spun,
And what we made to curse
We now would lean upon,
And feign kind Gods who perfect what man vainly tries.

Look, the world tempts our eye,
And we would know it all!
We map the starry sky,
We mine this earthen ball,
We measure the sea-tides, we number the sea-sands;

We scrutinise the dates
Of long-past human things,
The bounds of effaced states,
The lines of deceased kings;
We search out dead men's words, and works of dead
          men's hands;

We shut our eyes, and muse
How our own minds are made.
What springs of thought they use,

How righten'd, how betray'd –
And spend our wit to name what most employ
                    unnamed.

But still, as we proceed
The mass swells more and more
Of volumes yet to read,
Of secrets yet to explore.
Our hair grows grey, our eyes are dimm'd, our heat is
                    tamed;

We rest our faculties,
And thus address the Gods:
'True science if there is,
It stays in your abodes!
Man's measures cannot mete the immeasurable All.

'You only can take in
The world's immense design.
Our desperate search was sin,
Which henceforth we resign,
Sure only that your mind sees all things which befal.'

Fools! That in man's brief term
He cannot all things view,
Affords no ground to affirm
That there are Gods who do;

Nor does being weary prove that he has where to rest.

Again. – Our youthful blood
Claims rapture as its right;
The world, a rolling flood
Of newness and delight,
Draws in the enamoured gazer to its shining breast;

Pleasure, to our hot grasp,
Gives flowers, after flowers;
With passionate warmth we clasp
Hand after hand in ours;
Nor do we soon perceive how fast our youth is spent.

At once our eyes grow clear!
We see, in blank dismay,
Year posting after year,
Sense after sense decay;
Our shivering heart is mined by secret discontent;

Yet still, in spite of truth,
In spite of hopes entomb'd,
That longing of our youth
Burns ever unconsumed,
Still hungrier for delight as delights grow more rare.

We pause; we hush our heart,
And thus address the Gods:
'The world hath failed to impart

The joy our youth forebodes,
Fail'd to fill up the void which in our breasts we bear.


'Changeful till now, we still
    Look'd on to something new;
Let us, with changeless will,
    Henceforth look on to you,
To find with you the joy we in vain here require!'


Fools! That so often here
    Happiness mock'd our prayer,
I think might make us fear
    A like event elsewhere;
Make us, not fly to dreams, but moderate desire.


And yet, for those who know
    Themselves, who wisely take
Their way through life, and bow
    To what they cannot break,
Why should I say that life need yield but *moderate* bliss?


Shall we, with temper spoil'd,
    Health sapp'd by living ill,
And judgment all embroil'd
    By sadness and self-will,
Shall *we* judge what for man is not true bliss or is?

Is it so small a thing
To have enjoy'd the sun,
To have lived light in the spring,
To have loved, to have thought, to have done;
To have advanced true friends, and beat down baffling
          foes –

That we must feign a bliss
Of doubtful future date,
And, while we dream on this,
Lose all our present state,
And relegate to worlds yet distant our repose?

Not much, I know, you prize
What pleasures may be had,
Who look on life with eyes
Estranged, like mine, and sad:
And yet the village-churl feels the truth more than you,

Who's loth to leave this life
Which to him little yields –
His hard-task'd sunburnt wife, –
His often-labour'd fields,
The boors with whom he talk'd, the country-spots he
          knew.

But thou, because thou hear'st
Men scoff at Heaven and Fate,

Because the Gods thou fear'st
Fail to make blest thy state,
Tremblest, and wilt not dare to trust the joys there are!

I say: Fear not! Life still
Leaves human effort scope.
But, since life teems with ill,
Nurse no extravagant hope;
Because thou must not dream, thou need'st not then
despair!

from *Tristram and Iseult*

### III
*Iseult of Brittany*

A year had flown, and o'er the sea away,
In Cornwall, Tristram and Queen Iseult lay;
In King Marc's chapel, in Tyntagel old –
There in a ship they bore those lovers cold.
The young surviving Iseult, one bright day,
Had wander'd forth. Her children were at play
In a green circular hollow in the heath
Which borders the sea-shore – a country path
Creeps over it from the till'd fields behind.
The hollow's grassy banks are soft-inclined,
And to one standing on them, far and near
The lone unbroken view spreads bright and clear

Over the waste. This cirque of open ground
Is light and green; the heather, which all round
Creeps thickly, grows not here; but the pale grass
Is strewn with rocks, and many a shiver'd mass
Of vein'd white-gleaming quartz, and here and there
Dotted with holly-trees and juniper.
In the smooth centre of the opening stood
Three hollies side by side, and made a screen,
Warm with the winter-sun, of burnish'd green;
With scarlet berries gemm'd, the fell-fare's food.
Under the glittering hollies Iseult stands,
Watching her children play; their little hands
Are busy gathering spars of quartz, and streams
Of staghorn for their hats; anon, with screams
Of mad delight they drop their spoils, and bound
Among the holly-clumps and broken ground,
Racing full speed, and startling in their rush
The fell-fares and the speckled missel-thrush
Out of their glossy coverts; – but when now
Their cheeks were flush'd, and over each hot brow,
Under the feather'd hats of the sweet pair,
In blinding masses shower'd the golden hair –
Then Iseult call'd them to her, and the three
Cluster'd under the holly-screen, and she
Told them an old-world Breton history.

Warm in their mantles wrapt the three stood there,
Under the hollies, in the clear still air –

Mantles with those rich furs deep glistering
Which Venice ships do from swart Egypt bring.
Long they stay'd still – then, pacing at their ease,
Moved up and down under the glossy trees.
But still, as they pursued their warm dry road,
From Iseult's lips the unbroken story flow'd,
And still the children listen'd, their blue eyes
Fix'd on their mother's face in wide surprise;
Nor did their looks stray once to the sea-side,
Nor to the brown heaths round them, bright and
      wide,
Nor to the snow, which, though 't was all away
From the open heath, still by the hedgerows lay,
Nor to the shining sea-fowl, that with screams
Bore up from where the bright Atlantic gleams,
Swooping to landward; nor to where, quite clear,
The fell-fares settled on the thickets near.
And they would still have listen'd, till dark night
Came keen and chill down on the heather bright;
But, when the red glow on the sea grew cold,
And the grey turrets of the castle old
Look'd sternly through the frosty evening-air,
Then Iseult took by the hand those children fair,
And brought her tale to an end, and found the path,
And led them home over the darkening heath.

And is she happy? Does she see unmoved

The days in which she might have lived and loved

Slip without bringing bliss slowly away,
One after one, to-morrow like to-day?
Joy has not found her yet, nor ever will –
Is it this thought which makes her mien so still,
Her features so fatigued, her eyes, though sweet,
So sunk, so rarely lifted save to meet
Her children's? She moves slow; her voice alone
Hath yet an infantine and silver tone,
But even that comes languidly; in truth,
She seems one dying in a mask of youth.
And now she will go home, and softly lay
Her laughing children in their beds, and play
Awhile with them before they sleep; and then
She'll light her silver lamp, which fishermen
Dragging their nets through the rough waves, afar,
Along this iron coast, know like a star,
And take her broidery-frame, and there she'll sit
Hour after hour, her gold curls sweeping it;
Lifting her soft-bent head only to mind
Her children, or to listen to the wind.
And when the clock peals midnight, she will move
Her work away, and let her fingers rove
Across the shaggy brows of Tristram's hound
Who lies, guarding her feet, along the ground;
Or else she will fall musing, her blue eyes
Fixt, her slight hands clasp'd on her lap; then rise,
And at her prie-dieu kneel, until she have told
Her rosary-beads of ebony tipp'd with gold,

Then to her soft sleep – and to-morrow'll be
To-day's exact repeated effigy.

Yes, it is lonely for her in her hall.
The children, and the grey-hair'd seneschal,
Her women, and Sir Tristram's aged hound,
Are there the sole companions to be found.
But these she loves; and noisier life than this
She would find ill to bear, weak as she is.
She has her children, too, and night and day
Is with them; and the wide heaths where they play,
The hollies, and the cliff, and the sea-shore,
The sand, the sea-birds, and the distant sails,
These are to her dear as to them; the tales
With which this day the children she beguiled
She gleaned from Breton grandames, when a child,
In every hut along this sea-coast wild.
She herself loves them still, and, when they are told,
Can forget all to hear them, as of old.

Dear saints, it is not sorrow, as I hear,
Not suffering, which shuts up eye and ear
To all that has delighted them before,
And lets us be what we were once no more.
No, we may suffer deeply, yet retain
Power to be moved and soothed, for all our pain,
By what of old pleased us, and will again.
No, 'tis the gradual furnace of the world,

In whose hot air our spirits are upcurl'd
Until they crumble, or else grow like steel –
Which kills in us the bloom, the youth, the spring –
Which leaves the fierce necessity to feel,
But takes away the power – this can avail,
By drying up our joy in everything,
To make our former pleasures all seem stale.
This, or some tyrannous single thought, some fit
Of passion, which subdues our souls to it,
Till for its sake alone we live and move –
Call it ambition, or remorse, or love –
This too can change us wholly, and make seem
All which we did before, shadow and dream.

And yet, I swear, it angers me to see
How this fool passion gulls men potently;
Being, in truth, but a diseased unrest,
And an unnatural overheat at best.
How they are full of languor and distress
Not having it; which when they do possess,
They straightway are burnt up with fume and care,
And spend their lives in posting here and there
Where this plague drives them; and have little ease,
Are furious with themselves, and hard to please.
Like that bold Cæsar, the famed Roman wight,
Who wept at reading of a Grecian knight
Who made a name at younger years than he;
Or that renown'd mirror of chivalry,

Prince Alexander, Philip's peerless son,
Who carried the great war from Macedon
Into the Soudan's realm, and thundered on
To die at thirty-five in Babylon.

What tale did Iseult to the children say,
Under the hollies, that bright winter's day?

She told them of the fairy-haunted land
Away the other side of Brittany,
Beyond the heaths, edged by the lonely sea;
Of the deep forest-glades of Broce-liande,
Through whose green boughs the golden sunshine
        creeps,
Where Merlin by the enchanted thorn-tree sleeps.
For here he came with the fay Vivian,
One April, when the warm days first began.
He was on foot, and that false fay, his friend,
On her white palfrey; here he met his end,
In these lone sylvan glades, that April-day.
This tale of Merlin and the lovely fay
Was the one Iseult chose, and she brought clear
Before the children's fancy him and her.

Blowing between the stems, the forest-air
Had loosen'd the brown locks of Vivian's hair,
Which play'd on her flush'd cheek, and her blue eyes
28 Sparked with mocking glee and exercise.

Her palfrey's flanks were mired and bathed in sweat,
For they had travelled far and not stopp'd yet.
A brier in that tangled wilderness
Had scored her white right hand, which she allows
To rest ungloved on her green riding-dress;
The other warded off the drooping boughs.
But still she chatted on, with her blue eyes
Fix'd full on Merlin's face, her stately prize.
Her 'haviour had the morning's fresh clear grace,
The spirit of the woods was in her face.
She look'd so witching fair, that learned wight
Forgot his craft, and his best wits took flight;
And he grew fond, and eager to obey
His mistress, use her empire as she may.

They came to where the brushwood ceased, and day
Peer'd 'twixt the stems; and the ground broke away,
In a sloped sward down to a brawling brook;
And up as high as where they stood to look
On the brook's farther side was clear, but then
The underwood and trees began again.
This open glen was studded thick with thorns
Then white with blossom; and you saw the horns,
Through last year's fern, of the shy fallow-deer
Who come at noon down to the water here.
You saw the bright-eyed squirrels dart along
Under the thorns on the green sward; and strong
The blackbird whistled from the dingles near,

And the weird chipping of the woodpecker
Rang lonelily and sharp; the sky was fair,
And a fresh breath of spring stirr'd everywhere.
Merlin and Vivian stopp'd on the slope's brow,
To gaze on the light sea of leaf and bough
Which glistering plays all round them, lone and mild,
As if to itself the quiet forest smiled.
Upon the brow-top grew a thorn, and here
The grass was dry and moss'd, and you saw clear
Across the hollow; white anemonies
Starr'd the cool turf, and clumps of primroses
Ran out from the dark underwood behind.
No fairer resting-place a man could find.
'Here let us halt,' said Merlin then; and she
Nodded, and tied her palfrey to a tree.

They sate them down together, and a sleep
Fell upon Merlin, more like death, so deep.
Her finger on her lips, then Vivian rose,
And from her brown-lock'd head the wimple throws,
And takes it in her hand, and waves it over
The blossom'd thorn-tree and her sleeping lover.
Nine times she waved the fluttering wimple round,
And made a little plot of magic ground.
And in that daised circle, as men say,
Is Merlin prisoner till the judgment-day;
But she herself whither she will can rove –
For she was passing weary of his love.

# Dover Beach

The sea is calm to-night.
The tide is full, the moon lies fair
Upon the straits; – on the French coast the light
Gleams and is gone; the cliffs of England stand,
Glimmering and vast, out in the tranquil bay.
Come to the window, sweet is the night-air!
Only, from the long line of spray
Where the sea meets the moon-blanch'd land,
Listen! You hear the grating roar
Of pebbles which the waves draw back, and fling,
At their return, up the high strand,
Begin, and cease, and then again begin,
With tremulous cadence slow, and bring
The eternal note of sadness in.
Sophocles long ago
Heard it on the Aegaean, and it brought
Into his mind the turbid ebb and flow
Of human misery; we
Find also in the sound a thought,
Hearing it by this distant northern sea.

The Sea of Faith
Was once, too, at the full, and round earth's shore
Lay like the folds of a bright girdle furl'd.
But now I only hear

Its melancholy, long, withdrawing roar,
Retreating, to the breath
Of the night-wind, down the vast edges drear
And naked shingles of the world.

Ah, love, let us be true
To one another! for the world, which seems
To lie before us like a land of dreams,
So various, so beautiful, so new,
Hath really neither joy, nor love, nor light,
Nor certitude, nor peace, nor help for pain;
And we are here as on a darkling plain
Swept with confused alarms of struggle and flight,
Where ignorant armies clash by night.


## from *Sohrab and Rustum*

But the majestic river floated on,
Out of the mist and hum of that low land,
Into the frosty starlight, and there moved,
Rejoicing, through the hush'd Chorasmian waste,
Under the solitary moon; – he flow'd
Right for the polar star, past Orgunjè,
Brimming, and bright, and large; then sands begin
To hem his watery march, and dam his streams,
And split his currents; that for many a league
The shorn and parcell'd Oxus strains along;

Through beds of sand and matted rushy isles –
Oxus, forgetting the bright speed he had
In his high mountain-cradle in Pamere,
A foil'd circuitous wanderer – till at last
The long'd-for dash of waves is heard, and wide
His luminous home of waters opens, bright
And tranquil, from whose floor the new-bathed stars
Emerge, and shine upon the Aral Sea.

## The Scholar Gipsy

Go, for they call you, shepherd, from the hill;
  Go, shepherd, and untie the wattled cotes!
    No longer leave thy wistful flock unfed,
  Nor let thy bawling fellows rack their throats,
    Nor the cropp'd herbage shoot another head.
      But when the fields are still,
  And the tired men and dogs all gone to rest,
    And only the white sheep are sometimes seen
    Cross and recross the strips of moon-blanch'd
      green
Come, shepherd, and again begin the quest!

Here, where the reaper was at work of late –
  In this high field's dark corner, where he leaves
    His coat, his basket, and his earthen cruse,
  And in the sun all morning binds the sheaves,

Then here, at noon, comes back his stores to use –
    Here will I sit and wait,
While to my ear from uplands far away
    The bleating of the folded flocks is borne,
    With distant cries of reapers in the corn –
All the live murmur of a summer's day.

Screen'd is this nook o'er the high, half-reap'd field,
    And here till sun-down, shepherd! will I be.
    Through the thick corn the scarlet poppies peep,
And round green roots and yellowing stalks I see
    Pale pink convolvulus in tendrils creep;
        And air-swept lindens yield
Their scent, and rustle down their perfumed showers
    Of bloom on the bent grass where I am laid,
    And bower me from the August sun with shade;
And the eye travels down to Oxford's towers.

And near me on the grass lies Glanvil's book –
    Come, let me read the oft-read tale again!
    The story of the Oxford scholar poor,
Of pregnant parts and quick inventive brain,
    Who, tired of knocking at preferment's door,
        One summer-morn forsook
His friends, and went to learn the gipsy-lore,
    And roam'd the world with that wild brotherhood,
    And came, as most men deem'd, to little good,
But came to Oxford and his friends no more.

But once, years after, in the country-lanes,
    Two scholars, whom at college erst he knew,
        Met him, and of his way of life enquired;
    Whereat he answer'd, that the gipsy-crew,
        His mates, had arts to rule as they desired
            The workings of men's brains,
And they can bind them to what thoughts they will.
    'And I,' he said, 'the secret of their art,
        When fully learn'd, will to the world impart;
But it needs heaven-sent moments for this skill.'

This said, he left them, and return'd no more. –
    But rumours hung about the country-side,
        That the lost Scholar long was seen to stray,
    Seen by rare glimpses, pensive and tongue-tied,
        In hat of antique shape, and cloak of grey,
            The same the gipsies wore.
Shepherds had met him on the Hurst in spring;
    At some lone alehouse in the Berkshire moors,
        On the warm ingle-bench, the smock-frock'd boors
Had found him seated at their entering,

But, 'mid their drink and clatter, he would fly.
    And I myself seem half to know thy looks,
        And put the shepherds, wanderer! on thy trace;
    And boys who in lone wheatfields scare the rooks
        I ask if thou hast pass'd their quiet place;
            Or in my boat I lie

Moor'd to the cool bank in the summer-heats,
  'Mid wide grass meadows which the sunshine fills,
  And watch the warm, green-muffled Cumner hills,
And wonder if thou haunt'st their shy retreats.

For most, I know, thou lov'st retired ground!
  Thee at the ferry Oxford riders blithe,
    Returning home on summer-nights, have met
  Crossing the stripling Thames at Bab-lock-hithe,
    Trailing in the cool stream thy fingers wet,
      As the punt's rope chops round;
  And leaning backward in a pensive dream,
    And fostering in thy lap a heap of flowers
    Pluck'd in shy fields and distant Wychwood
        bowers,
  And thine eyes resting on the moonlit stream.

And then they land, and thou are seen no more! –
  Maidens, who from the distant hamlets come
    To dance around the Fyfield elm in May,
  Oft through the darkening fields have seen thee
        roam,
    Or cross a stile into the public way.
      Oft thou hast given them store
  Of flowers – the frail-leaf'd, white anemony,
    Dark bluebells drench'd with dews of summer eves,
    And purple orchises with spotted leaves –
  But none hath words she can report of thee.

And, above Godstow Bridge, when hay-time's here
    In June, and many a scythe in sunshine flames,
        Men who through those wide fields of breezy grass
    Where black-wing'd swallows haunt the glittering
            Thames,
        To bathe in the abandon'd lasher pass,
            Have often pass'd thee near
    Sitting upon the river bank o'ergrown;
        Mark'd thine outlandish garb, thy figure spare,
        Thy dark vague eyes, and soft abstracted air –
    But, when they came from bathing, thou wast gone!

At some lone homestead in the Cumner hills,
    Where at her open door the housewife darns,
        Thou hast been seen, or hanging on a gate
    To watch the threshers in the mossy barns.
        Children, who early range these slopes and late
            For cresses from the rills,
    Have known thee eyeing, all an April-day,
        The springing pastures and the feeding kine;
        And mark'd thee, when the stars come out and
            shine,
    Through the long dewy grass move slow away.

In autumn, on the skirts of Bagley Wood –
    Where most the gipsies by the turf-edged way
        Pitch their smoked tents, and every bush you see
    With scarlet patches tagg'd and shreds of grey,

Above the forest-ground called Thessaly –
　　The blackbird, picking food,
Sees thee, nor stops his meal, nor fears at all;
　　So often has he known thee past him stray,
　　Rapt, twirling in thy hand a wither'd spray,
And waiting for the spark from heaven to fall.


And once, in winter, on the causeway chill
　　Where home through flooded fields foot-travellers go,
　　　Have I not pass'd thee on the wooden bridge,
Wrapt in thy cloak and battling with the snow,
　　　Thy face tow'rd Hinksey and its wintry ridge?
　　　　And thou hast climb'd the hill,
And gain'd the white brow of the Gumner range;
　　　Turn'd once to watch, while thick the snowflakes
　　　　fall,
　　　The line of festal light in Christ-Church hall –
Then sought thy straw in some sequestered grange.


But what – I dream! Two hundred years are flown
　　Since first thy story ran through Oxford halls,
　　　And the grave Glanvil did the tale inscribe
That thou wert wander'd from the studious walls
　　　To learn strange arts, and join a gipsy-tribe;
　　　　And thou from earth art gone
Long since, and in some quiet churchyard laid –
　　　Some country-nook, where o'er thy unknown grave

Tall grasses and white flowering nettles wave,
   Under a dark, red-fruited yew-tree's shade.

– No, no, thou hast not felt the lapse of hours!
   For what wears out the life of mortal men?
      'Tis that from change to change their being rolls;
      'Tis that repeated shocks, again, again,
         Exhaust the energy of strongest souls
            And numb the elastic powers.
   Till having used our nerves with bliss and teen,
      And tired upon a thousand schemes our wit,
      To the just-pausing Genius we remit
   Our worn-out life, and are – what we have been.

Thou hast not lived, why should'st thou perish, so?
   Thou hadst *one* aim, *one* business, *one* desire;
      Else wert thou long since number'd with the dead!
   Else hadst thou spent, like other men, thy fire!
      The generations of thy peers are fled,
         And we ourselves shall go;
   But thou possessest an immortal lot,
      And we imagine thee exempt from age
      And living as thou liv'st on Glanvil's page,
   Because thou hadst – what we, alas! have not.

For early didst thou leave the world, with powers
   Fresh, undiverted to the world without,
      Firm to their mark, not spent on other things;

Free from the sick fatigue, the languid doubt,
    Which much to have tried, in much been baffled,
        brings.
        O life unlike to ours!
Who fluctuate idly without term or scope,
    Of whom each strives, nor knows for what he
        strives,
    And each half lives a hundred different lives;
Who wait like thee, but not, like thee, in hope.

Thou waitest for the spark from heaven! and we,
    Light half-believers of our casual creeds,
        Who never deeply felt, nor clearly will'd,
    Whose insight never has borne fruit in deeds,
        Whose vague resolves never have been fulfilled;
            For whom each year we see
    Breeds new beginnings, disappointments new;
        Who hesitate and falter life away,
        And lose to-morrow the ground won to-day –
Ah! do not we, wanderer! await it too?

Yes, we await it! – but it still delays,
    And then we suffer! and amongst us one,
        Who most has suffer'd, takes dejectedly
            His seat upon the intellectual throne;
        And all his store of sad experience he
    Lays bare of wretched days;

Tells us his misery's birth and growth and signs,

And how the dying spark of hope was fed,
    And how the breast was soothed, and how the
        head,
And all his hourly varied anodynes.


This for our wisest! and we others pine,
    And wish the long unhappy dream would end,
        And waive all claim to bliss, and try to bear;
    With close-lipp'd patience for our only friend,
        Sad patience, too near neighbour to despair –
            But none has hope like thine!
    Thou through the fields and through the woods dost
        stray,
        Roaming the country-side, a truant boy,
        Nursing thy project in unclouded joy,
    And every doubt long blown by time away.


O born in days when wits were fresh and clear,
    And life ran gaily as the sparkling Thames;
        Before this strange disease of modern life,
    With its sick hurry, its divided aims,
        Its heads o'ertax'd, its palsied hearts, was rife –
            Fly hence, our contact fear!
    Still fly, plunge deeper in the bowering wood!
        Averse, as Dido did with gesture stern
        From her false friend's approach in Hades turn,
    Wave us away, and keep thy solitude!

Still nursing the unconquerable hope,
   Still clutching the inviolable shade,
      With a free, onward impulse brushing through,
   By night, the silver'd branches of the glade
      Far on the forest-skirts, where none pursue,
         On some mild pastoral slope
   Emerge, and resting on the moonlit pales
   Freshen thy flowers as in former years
      With dew, or listen with enchanted ears,
From the dark dingles, to the nightingales!

But fly our paths, our feverish contact fly!
   For strong the infection of our mental strife,
      Which, though it gives no bliss, yet spoils for rest;
         And we should win thee from thy own fair life,
      Like us distracted, and like us unblest.
   Soon, soon thy cheer would die,
   Thy hopes grow timorous, and unfix'd thy powers,
      And thy clear aims be cross and shifting made;
      And then thy glad perennial youth would fade,
Fade, and grow old at last, and die like ours.

Then fly our greetings, fly our speech and smiles!
   – As some grave Tyrian trader, from the sea,
      Descried at sunrise an emerging prow
   Lifting the cool-hair'd creepers stealthily,
      The fringes of a southward-facing brow
Among the Aegaean isles;

And saw the merry Grecian coaster come,
  Freighted with amber grapes, and Chian wine,
  Green, bursting figs, and tunnies steep'd in brine
And knew the intruders on his ancient home,

The young light-hearted masters of the waves
  And snatch'd his rudder, and shook out more sail;
  And day and night held on indignantly
O'er the blue Midland waters with the gale,
  Betwixt the Syrtes and soft Sicily,
    To where the Atlantic raves
Outside the western straits; and unbent sails
  There, where down cloudy cliffs, through sheets of
    foam,
  Shy traffickers, the dark Iberians come;
And on the beach undid his corded bales.

### Requiescat

Strew on her roses, roses,
  And never a spray of yew!
In quiet she reposes;
  Ah, would that I did too!

Her mirth the world required;
  She bathed it in smiles of glee.

But her heart was tired, tired,
    And now they let her be.

Her life was turning, turning,
    In mazes of heat and sound.
But for peace her soul was yearning,
    And now peace laps her round.

Her cabin'd, ample spirit,
    It flutter'd and fail'd for breath.
To-night it doth inherit
    The vasty hall of death.


## *Thyrsis*

A MONODY, *to commemorate the author's friend,*
ARTHUR HUGH CLOUGH, *who died at Florence, 1861*

How changed is here each spot man makes or fills!
    In the two Hinkseys nothing keeps the same;
        The village street its haunted mansion lacks,
    And from the sign is gone Sibylla's name,
        And from the roofs the twisted chimney-stacks –
        Are ye too changed, ye hills?
    See, 'tis no foot of unfamiliar men
        To-night from Oxford up your pathway strays!
        Here came I often, often, in old days –
44    Thyrsis and I; we still had Thyrsis then.

Runs it not here, the track by Childsworth Farm,
   Past the high wood, to where the elm-tree crowns
      The hill behind whose ridge the sunset flames?
The signal-elm, that looks on Ilsley Downs,
   The Vale, the three lone weirs, the youthful
         Thames;
      This winter-eve is warm,
Humid the air! leafless, yet soft as spring,
   The tender purple spray on copse and briers!
      And that sweet city with her dreaming-spires,
She needs not June for beauty's heightening,

Lovely all times she lies, lovely to-night! –
   Only, methinks, some loss of habit's power
      Befalls me wandering through this upland dim.
Once pass'd I blindfold here, at any hour;
      Now seldom come I, since I came with him.
         That single elm-tree bright
Against the west – I miss it! is it gone?
   We prized it dearly; while it stood, we said;
      Our friend, the Gipsy-Scholar, was not dead;
While the tree lived, he in these fields lived on.

Too rare, too rare, grow now my visits here,
   But once I knew each field, each flower, each stick;
      And with the country-folk acquaintance made
By barn in threshing-time, by new-built rick.
      Here, too, our shepherd-pipes we first assay'd.                45

Ah me! this many a year
My pipe is lost, my shepherd's holiday!
Needs must I lose them, needs with heavy heart
Into the world and wave of men depart;
But Thyrsis of his own will went away.


It irk'd him to be here, he could not rest.
He loved each simple joy the country yields,
He loved his mates; but yet he could not keep,
For that a shadow lour'd on the fields,
Here with the shepherds and the silly sheep.
Some life of men unblest
He knew, which made him droop, and filled his head.
He went; his piping took a troubled sound
Of storms that rage outside our happy ground;
He could not wait their passing, he is dead.


So, some tempestuous morn in early June,
When the year's primal burst of bloom is o'er,
Before the roses and the longest day –
When garden-walks and all the grassy floor
With blossoms red and white of fallen May
And chestnut-flowers are strewn
So have I heard the cuckoo's parting cry,
From the wet field, through the vext garden-trees,
Come with the volleying rain and tossing breeze:
*The bloom is gone, and with the bloom go I!*

Too quick despairer, wherefore wilt thou go?
  Soon will the high Midsummer pomps come on,
    Soon will the musk carnations break and swell,
  Soon shall we have gold-dusted snapdragon,
    Sweet-William with his homely cottage-smell,
      And stocks in fragrant blow;
  Roses that down the alleys shine afar,
    And open, jasmine-muffled lattices,
    And groups under the dreaming garden-trees,
  And the full moon, and the white evening-star.

He harkens not! light comer, he is flown!
  What matters it? next year he will return,
    And we shall have him in the sweet spring-
        days,
  With whitening hedges, and uncrumpling fern,
    And blue-bells trembling by the forest-ways,
      And scent of hay new-mown.
  But Thyrsis never more we swains shall see;
    See him come back, and cut a smoother reed,
    And blow a strain the world at last shall heed –
  For Time, not Corydon, hath conquer'd thee!

Alack, for Corydon no rival now! –
  But when Sicilian shepherds lost a mate,
    Some good survivor with his flute would go,
  Piping a ditty sad for Bion's fate;
    And cross the unpermitted ferry's flow,

And relax Pluto's brow,
And make leap up with joy the beauteous head
    Of Proserpine, among whose crowned hair
    Are flowers first open'd on Sicilian air,
And flute his friend, like Orpheus, from the
        dead.


O easy access to the hearer's grace
    When Dorian shepherds sang to Proserpine!
        For she herself had trod Sicilian fields,
    She knew the Dorian water's gush divine,
        She knew each lily white which Enna yields,
            Each rose with blushing face;
    She loved the Dorian pipe, the Dorian strain.
        But ah, of our poor Thames she never heard!
        Her foot the Cumner cowslips never stirr'd;
    And we should tease her with our plaint in vain!


Well! wind-dispersed and vain the words will be,
    Yet, Thyrsis, let me give my grief its hour
        In the old haunt, and find our tree-topp'd hill!
    Who, if not I, for questing here hath power?
        I know the wood which hides the daffodil,
            I know the Fyfield tree,
    I know what white, what purple fritillaries
        The grassy harvest of the river-fields,
            Above by Ensham, down by Sandford, yields,
    And what sedged brooks are Thames's tributaries;

I know these slopes; who knows them if not I? –
    But many a dingle on the loved hill-side,
        With thorns once studded, old, white-blossom'd
            trees,
    Where thick the cowslips grew, and far descried
      High tower'd the spikes of purple orchises,
        Hath since our day put by
The coronals of that forgotten time;
    Down each green bank hath gone the ploughboy's
        team,
    And only in the hidden brookside gleam
Primroses, orphans of the flowery prime.

Where is the girl, who by the boatman's door,
    Above the locks, above the boating throng,
      Unmoor'd our skiff when through the Wytham
        flats,
    Red loosestrife and blond meadow-sweet among
      And darting swallows and light water-gnats,
        We track'd the shy Thames shore?
Where are the mowers, who, as the tiny swell
    Of our boat passing heaved the river-grass,
    Stood with suspended scythe to see us pass? –
They all are gone, and thou art gone as well!

Yes, thou art gone! and round me too the night
    In ever-nearing circle weaves her shade.
    I see her veil draw soft across the day,

I feel her slowly chilling breath invade
   The cheek grown thin, the brown hair sprent with
      grey;
     I feel her finger light
Laid pausefully upon life's headlong train; –
   The foot less prompt to meet the morning dew,
   The heart less bounding at emotion new,
And hope, once crush'd, less quick to spring again.

And long the way appears, which seem'd so short
   To the less practised eye of sanguine youth;
     And high the mountain-tops, in cloudy air,
The mountain-tops where is the throne of Truth,
     Tops in life's morning-sun so bright and bare!
      Unbreachable the fort.
Of the long-batter'd world uplifts its wall;
   And strange and vain the earthly turmoil grows,
   And near and real the charm of thy repose,
And night as welcome as a friend would fall.

But hush! the upland hath a sudden loss
   Of quiet! – Look, adown the dusk hill-side,
     A troop of Oxford hunters going home,
As in old days, jovial and talking, ride!
     From hunting with the Berkshire hounds they come
      Quick! let me fly, and cross
Into yon farther field! – 'Tis done; and see,
     Back'd by the sunset, which doth glorify

The orange and pale violet evening-sky,
   Bare on its lonely ridge, the Tree! the Tree!

I take the omen! Eve lets down her veil,
   The white fog creeps from bush to bush about,
      The west unflushes, the high stars grow bright,
And in the scatter'd farms the lights come out.
      I cannot reach the signal-tree to-night,
         Yet, happy omen, hail!
   Hear it from thy broad lucent Arno-vale
      (For there thine earth-forgetting eyelids keep
      The morningless and unawakening sleep
Under the flowery oleanders pale),

Hear it, O Thyrsis, still our tree is there! –
   Ah, vain! These English fields, this upland dim,
      These brambles pale with mist engarlanded,
That lone, sky-pointing tree, are not for him;
      To a boon southern country he is fled,
         And now in happier air,
   Wandering with the great Mother's train divine
      (And purer or more subtle soul than thee,
      I trow, the mighty Mother doth not see)
Within a folding of the Apennine,

Thou hearest the immortal chants of old! –
   Putting his sickle to the perilous grain
      In the hot cornfield of the Phrygian king,

For thee the Lityerses-song again
　　Young Daphnis with his silver voice doth sing;
　　　Sings his Sicilian fold,
His sheep, his hapless love, his blinded eyes –
　　And how a call celestial round him rang,
　　And heavenward from the fountain-brink he
　　　　sprang,
And all the marvel of the golden skies.

There thou art gone, and me thou leavest here
　　Sole in these fields! yet will I not despair.
　　　Despair I will not, while I yet descry
Neath the mild canopy of English air
　　That lonely tree against the western sky.
　　　Still, still these slopes, 'tis clear,
Our Gipsy-Scholar haunts, outliving thee!
　　Fields where soft sheep from cages pull the hay,
　　Woods with anemonies in flower till May,
Know him a wanderer still; then why not me?

A fugitive and gracious light he seeks,
　　Shy to illumine; and I seek it too.
　　　This does not come with houses or with gold,
With place, with honour, and a flattering crew;
　　　'Tis not in the world's market bought and sold –
　　　But the smooth-slipping weeks
Drop by, and leave its seeker still untired;
　　Out of the heed of mortals he is gone,

He wends unfollow'd, he must house alone;
Yet on he fares, by his own heart inspired.

Thou too, O Thyrsis, on like quest wast bound;
Thou wanderedst with me for a little hour!
Men gave thee nothing; but this happy quest,
If men esteem'd thee feeble, gave thee power,
If men procured thee trouble, gave thee rest.
And this rude Cumner ground,
Its fir-topped Hurst, its farms, its quiet fields,
Here cam'st thou in thy jocund youthful time,
Here was thine height of strength, thy golden prime
And still the haunt beloved a virtue yields.

What though the music of thy rustic flute
Kept not for long its happy, country tone;
Lost it too soon, and learnt a stormy note
Of men contention-tost, of men who groan,
Which task'd thy pipe too sore, and tired thy
throat –
It fail'd, and thou wast mute!
Yet hadst thou alway visions of our light,
And long with men of care thou couldst not stay,
And soon thy foot resumed its wandering way,
Left human haunt, and on alone till night.

Too rare, too rare, grow now my visits here!
'Mid city-noise, not, as with thee of yore,

Thyrsis! in reach of sheep-bells is my home.
– Then through the great town's harsh, heart-
      wearying roar,
  Let in thy voice a whisper often come,
    To chase fatigue and fear:
*Why faintest thou? I wandered till I died.*
  *Roam on! The light we sought is shining still.*
   *Dost thou ask proof? Our tree yet crowns the hill,*
*Our Scholar travels yet the loved hill-side.*


## Growing Old

What is it to grow old?
Is it to lose the glory of the form,
The lustre of the eye?
Is it for beauty to forgo her wreath?
– Yes, but not this alone.

Is it to feel our strength –
Not our bloom only, but our strength – decay?
Is it to feel each limb
Grow stiffer, every function less exact,
Each nerve more loosely strung?

Yes, this, and more; but not
Ah, 'tis not what in youth we dreamed 'twould be!
'Tis not to have our life

Mellowed and softened as with sunset-glow,
A golden day's decline.

'Tis not to see the world
As from a height, with rapt prophetic eyes,
And heart profoundly stirred;
And weep, and feel the fullness of the past,
The years that are no more.

It is to spend long days
And not once feel that we were ever young;
It is to add, immured
In the hot prison of the present, month
To month with weary pain.

It is to suffer this,
And feel but half, and feebly, what we feel.
Deep in our hidden heart
Festers the dull remembrance of a change,
But no emotion – none.

It is – last stage of all –
When we are frozen up within, and quite
The phantom of ourselves,
To hear the world applaud the hollow ghost
Which blamed the living man.

# A Note on Matthew Arnold

Matthew Arnold (1822–88), English poet and critic, born at Laleham, Middlesex, on Christmas Eve, son of Thomas Arnold, the famous headmaster of Rugby School. From Rugby he won a scholarship to Balliol College, Oxford, in 1841. He was already interested in literature, his poem, *Alaric at Rome* having been printed at Rugby in 1840, and at Oxford in 1843 he won the Newdigate prize with a poem on Cromwell. The next year he took a second-class degree and for a short time taught classics at Rugby. In 1845 he was given a fellowship at Oriel College, and in 1846 travelled in France and Switzerland. He became private secretary to Lord Lansdowne (1847), a moderate Whig leader on whom Arnold, to a large extent, modelled his politics.

In 1849 appeared *The Strayed Reveller and Other Poems. By A.*; it attracted so little attention that the edition was withdrawn hastily, yet it contained, along with a number of poems of little merit, much that has won a lasting place in English literature, including 56 'Resignation' and 'The Forsaken Merman'. *Empedocles* on *Etna and Other Poems*, published in 1852, also under the initial A, was similarly quickly withdrawn.

In 1851, Arnold had been appointed by Lord Lansdowne an inspector of schools, and in this capacity he did a great deal for English education, although the drudgery involved proved to be a strain, and affected his output as a creative writer. Theories on why Arnold accepted the post vary from his need for a regular income (he married Frances Lucy in 1851), to a deliberate philosophic choice of a routine career. He produced valuable official reports on various foreign tours of inspection, admiring the German system of education; he remarked that the French university lacked liberty, the English science, but the German neither. Many of his advocated reforms were carried out, both in schools and universities.

In 1853 Arnold published under his own name an essay embodying his theory of poetry, together with a collection of poems, many already previously published. In 1857 he was appointed to the chair of poetry at Oxford, which he retained for ten years, and in 1867 published *New Poems*; this included 'Thyrsis' (on the death of his friend Arthur Hugh Clough) and gave Arnold a leading place as a poet. After 1867, however, he wrote little verse, concentrating on his prose writings. His *Essays in Criticism* (first series, 1865, second series, 1888), and *Culture and Anarchy*, by far his most important prose work, containing his best social commentary 57 and liveliest writing, greatly widened the bounds of literary criticism. Arnold felt that Victorian society could be saved from its materialism by the humanising medium of literary culture. The educating influence of its 'sweetness and light' was above all needed by the middle classes, whom Arnold called the philistines. He saw the poet's function as related to that of religion, and attacked contemporary Christian orthodoxy in *Literature and Dogma*, 1873, which aroused bitter opposition; he also considered the Bible important as poetry, applying to it standards of literary criticism. In 1883 he received an annual pension of £250, and the same year lectured in the United States. He died in Liverpool in 1888, and was buried at Laleham.

Among Arnold's best-known poems are 'Sohrab and Rustum', 'Dover Beach', and 'The Scholar Gipsy'.

# *Other titles in this series*